Just My Style

Just My Style

Published and Copyrighted © by
Malka Touger

5763 - 2003

Distributed by
Judaica Press Inc.
123 Ditmas Ave.
Brooklyn, N.Y. 11218
718-972-6200
800-972-6201
web: www.judaicapress.com
email: info@judaicapress.com

Acknowledgements:
Edited by Esther Chachamtzedek
Artwork and cover by Orit Martin
Layout and typography by Etti Benzriham
Special thanks to Rabbi Pesach Eliyahu Falk whose classic work,
עוז והדר לבושה, was an inspiration and a resource for
this text.

Comments and suggestions may be sent to: emetpub@gmail.com

Printed in Israel

CONTENTS

TZNIUS –
OUR WAY OF LIFE

Mrs. Rubin was shopping with her daughter, Chanie. "That's very nice," she said as Chanie posed in front of the mirror. "The color suits you and that outfit has a well dressed and **modest** look."

"I enjoyed Moshe Green's Bar Mitzvah last night," Mr. Stein commented to his wife. "It was a dignified, yet **modest** affair."

All the girls in Shevie's class like her. She is studious, talented, good hearted and **modest**.

Is it surprising to find that clothes, a party, and people can all be called modest?
- When Mrs. Rubin was complimenting her daughter's looks, she could have said: "...it has a well dressed look and is in accordance with Halachah."
- Mr. Stein could have said: "...it was a dignified, yet not lavish affair."
- We can describe Shevie as a girl who does not put on airs.

Yet instead, the word modest is used again and again. The Hebrew word for modesty is *tznius*. *Tznius* comes from the root: *tzena*, which means hidden. When something is hidden, it requires us to look deeper. *Tznius* is a way of life that helps us look deeper inside ourselves, others, and the world around us.

• When Mrs. Rubin said: "...the outfit has a modest look" she meant that when people would see Chanie wearing it, they would notice that her clothing does not distract from who she is **inside**.

• When Mr. Stein commented on the Green's Bar Mitzvah, he meant to say that the dignity of the event did not come from fancy table arrangements but that he enjoyed the joy and **actual content** of the *simchah*.

• One of the things that makes Shevie likeable, is that her fine qualities come from **within**.

We can see that *tznius* is much more than covering your knees and elbows. It is many things that are all part of a way of life that enables us to focus on what is real. This is the right way to live. It is the Jewish way. For men, women, boys and girls. In this reader we are going to speak mostly about *tznius* for girls.

DO YOU THINK IT IS BETTER TO USE THE WORD MODESTY OR TZNIUS, WHEN WE ARE DISCUSSING THIS TOPIC?

The prophet says: הַצְנֵעַ לֶכֶת עִם אֱלֹקֶיךָ - "What does *Hashem* require of you but to do justice, to love kindness, and to walk modestly with your G-d?" (*Michah* 6:8). With these words, Michah is summarizing the way Jewish people should live their lives. He is not mentioning *tznius* simply as one of the 613 *mitzvos*, but rather as a guideline for our way of life.

Ruth, the great-great-grandmother of David *haMelech,* learned about the *tzanua* way of life from her mother-in-law, Naomi. Ruth was sincere. "I will go with you wherever you go," she told Naomi. "I want to live the way you live."

"Do you know what this means?" Naomi asked the former princess of Moav. "Our life is so different."

Naomi explained many of the *halachos* of Jewish life to Ruth. As she described the lifestyle of a Jewish girl, she said: "**It is not the way** of Jewish girls to attend non-Jewish theaters and circuses" (*Ruth Rabbah* 2:22). Instead of only teaching her that we should

not go to such places of entertainment, Naomi was explaining to Ruth that those kinds of activities are not **our way** of life. Being Jewish does not mean simply doing what we are commanded and not doing what is forbidden; it means living the Jewish way. Like Ruth, we need to learn and remember that *tznius* is not merely wearing what is proper. **It is our way of life**.

TZNIUS IS DESCRIBED AS OUR WAY OF LIFE. WHAT AREAS DO YOU THINK IT INCLUDES?

NAOMI TOLD RUTH THAT THE JEWISH WAY IS DIFFERENT. SOME PEOPLE FEEL THAT BEING DIFFERENT CAN BE CHALLENGING. WHAT DO YOU THINK? HOW CAN WE MEET THAT CHALLENGE?

"I admit, we must have been an interesting sight," relates Mimi. "There we were at Hershy's Amusement Park, a group of counselors, appropriately dressed, taking charge of over one hundred campers dressed in tank tops, for whom this summer camp is their only exposure to Yiddishkeit.

"After a couple of hours on the rides, all the groups met and we began guiding the campers in washing their hands for lunch. As I was waiting with my group near the fountains, a woman walked over to me.

"'You know,' she said, 'I really respect you people. You're dedicated to your way of life and follow your rules strictly regardless of what other people think. It's only a shame that the little ones find it so hard to be different and don't want to keep your traditions.'

"I didn't know quite what to make of her statements. Should I explain to her that most of the 'little ones' she was referring to were children who had never

even been exposed to true Yiddishkeit?

"The woman must have noticed my perplexed look, for she quickly resumed her praises.

"'Never mind the young ones,' she said enthusiastically. 'You girls certainly have my vote. I mean, it must be so hard to stick to your Amish customs in the twenty-first century in America. G-d bless you teenagers.'

"I almost burst out laughing. Amish! So that's who she thought we were. What would have given her that notion? Then it dawned on me. All of us, though not intentionally, were wearing long black skirts, our camp tee-shirt had long sleeves with a small logo on the back that wasn't easily noticed and our hair was tied back neatly.

"Suppressing a chuckle, I replied, 'You're quite right about most everything you said. We are dedicated, we do follow our customs with determination, it's not always easy, and G-d certainly blesses us. But we are not Amish. We are Jewish, and we belong to a people who has been living this way from creation up to the twenty-first century and will continue doing so.

"The woman furrowed her brow and looked me over from head to toe. She was taken aback. 'Jewish?' she asked in surprise. She was silent for a moment as if contemplating her reply. Then she said almost in a whisper, 'I'm Jewish too. My parents came to the States from Europe after the war, but died soon after I was born. I was sent to an orphanage where some devoted and caring Amish people looked after me. I never met any real Jewish people.' Then the woman began to cry.

"I knew this was no coincidence. Being taken for Amish by this lonely Jewish woman was no longer amusing. It was a clear sign from above that I had a responsibility to help her reconnect to her Jewish roots. I took her name and address and this began, in the woman's words: 'a wonderful journey back home.'

"And to think it all came to be because of our tznius appearance...."

IN HIGH ESTEEM, IT'S A CENTRAL THEME

"I understand that *tznius* is important," says Rivki, "but there are 613 *mitzvos* in the Torah. Why does everyone always keep talking about *tznius*? My mother smothers me with *tznius* ideas, my teachers preach, my counselor counsels, and my neighbors labor on the topic. You'd think this is the whole basis of *Yiddishkeit*!"

Well, perhaps it is.

The *Midrash* (*Bereishis Rabbah* 18:2) says: After *Hashem* created Adam, He considered the different parts from which He would form Chavah. He said:

I will not create her from the head - so she should not be light-headed or high-headed and haughty;

Not from the eye - so she should not pry and look where unnecessary;

Not from the ear- so she should not be eager to hear gossip;

Not from the mouth - so she should not be a chitchat;

Not from the heart - so she should not be desirous and jealous;

Not from the hand - so she should not reach out where improper;

Not from the foot - so she should not venture out where inappropriate.

From where shall I create her?

From a very private place in the body: from an internal limb, the rib - so she will be *tznuah*.

ADAM'S BODY WAS CREATED FROM THE EARTH. DO
YOU THINK THERE MAY BE A MESSAGE IN THAT TO A
JEW? CAN THIS BE OF ANY ASSISTANCE IN LIVING A
LIFE OF TZNIUS?

Shortly after creation came the episode in *Gan Eden. Hashem* instructed Adam and Chavah to serve Him; they could eat from all types of fruit, but not from the עֵץ הדעת. After they sinned, *Hashem* clothed them, thereby teaching all of mankind about *tznius*. This was the first act immediately following חֵטְא עֵץ הַדַעַת. Why? Why *tznius* and why right then?

In the beginning, טוֹב and רַע were separate. The עֵץ הַדַעַת, which was off limits, was very clearly separate from all the other trees. This symbolized that life in *Gan Eden* did not demand an ongoing struggle of choosing between right and wrong. It was clear what should not be done and it was just a matter of staying away from that. After חֵטְא עֵץ הַדַעַת, things changed. The טוֹב and the רַע were no longer separate. It was as if the tree was not clearly marked and standing forbidden out there. Man and woman now had to deal with the יֵצֶר הַרַע and the יֵצֶר הַטוֹב that were now competing inside of them. Now it became harder to make the decision to do the right thing.

How do we overcome these challenges? If good and bad are not so clearly separated, how do we choose properly and do the right thing?

All that followed after חֵטְא עֵץ הַדַעַת, the entire Torah, was intended to do just that: teach us how to live in this world and chose what *Hashem* wants. Directly after the sin, *Hashem* clothed Adam and Chavah. The first thing mankind needed to learn was *tznius. Hashem* is saying: "This way of life, the *tznius* way, is the way you will be able to deal with the challenges you will now have to meet." *Tznius* is *Hashem*'s gift which empowers us to live a Torah life.

HOW CAN TZNIUS BE AN IMPORTANT FACTOR
IN KEEPING OTHER MITZVOS?

Along with *Hashem*'s instruction to be *tzanua*, He also ingrained in us a sensitivity to *tznius* - especially to women and girls.

The wisdom of Shlomoh haMelech spread far and wide. Word reached the African kingdom of Sheba and the Queen was both curious and skeptical. "I'll go check for myself," she decided. "I will challenge him with hard questions and riddles and see if he is as wise as everyone claims." She set out for Yerushalayim and gained an audience with the king.

One of the riddles was almost like a performance! The queen presented a group of children, who were about the same age and height, before the king; they were all dressed alike and had the same haircut - even their facial features were similar.

"Can you point out which are the boys and which are the girls?" she asked.

Shlomoh haMelech ordered a servant to set bowls of nuts and roasted seeds before the children. "Help yourselves," the king said. "Have as much as you'd like and take some for later, too."

In a short time he had an answer for the Queen of Sheba. How did he know?

Everyone could see.

All the boys lifted the corner of their robes, creating a kind of pocket, which they filled with nuts. But the girls would not lift their robes. Instead, they used kerchiefs to collect the snacks.

(*Midrash Shochar Tov, Mishlei* 1)

CAN WE RELY ON THIS INGRAINED NATURAL SENSITIVITY TO TZNIUS TO GUIDE US?

TZNIUS SHOWS, IN OUR LOOKS AND CLOTHES

If *tznius* is about our entire way of life, why is so much attention given to the *tznius* of our looks and our clothes?

"My mother is very 'uppity' about *tznius*," Mimi says. "Button up that shirt, zip up that top, pull up those socks, straighten up your hair. Sometimes it's hard to 'down' all this uplifting!"

Mimi is right when she uses the word "uplifting." The attention we pay to the *tznius* of our appearance is our way of uplifting ourselves from the lower standards of the world. The way we constantly move upward is by living a life of *tznius*, and what we wear and how we look are an important part.

Why?

Perhaps you have heard the common expression: "The clothes make the man." As Jews we know this is true, not because many people say so, but because the Torah tells us about the role clothes play. The Torah goes into great detail describing the clothes of the *kohanim*. Our Sages tell us that wearing those clothes has a very positive influence on a *kohen*:

בִּזְמַן שֶׁבִּגְדֵיהֶם עֲלֵיהֶם - כְּהוּנָתָם עֲלֵיהֶם, אֵין בִּגְדֵיהֶם עֲלֵיהֶם - אֵין כְּהוּנָתָם עֲלֵיהֶם

"When the *kohanim* wear their special clothes, their *kehunah* rests upon them in a complete

way. When they do not wear their clothes, they do not have the full *kedushah* of the *kehunah*" (*Zevachim* 17b). We see that the *kohen*'s clothing adds to his holiness.

Like the requirements of *tznius* for our clothing, the *kohen*'s garments had to be just the right length for him - not too long and not too short. The Torah says: וְלָבַשׁ הַכֹּהֵן מִדּוֹ בַד - "And the *kohen* shall wear his fitted linen tunic" (*Vayikra* 6:3). The word מִדּוֹ can be understood as מַדִּים, which means uniform, or as מִידָה, which means measurement.

David *haMelech* describes Jewish women and girls as daughters of a king, and says: מִמִּשְׁבְּצוֹת זָהָב לְבוּשָׁה - "Her garments are like those that have golden settings" (*Tehillim* 45:14). This reminds us of the clothes of the *Kohen Gadol* because the stones of the *choshen,* the breastplate, were set in gold.

When Shlomoh *haMelech* praises the Jewish woman, he reminds her of the role clothes play in the service of *Hashem*. He writes: שֵׁשׁ וְאַרְגָּמָן לְבוּשָׁה - "Linen and purple wool are her clothing" (*Mishlei* 31:22), for linen and purple wool were used in the sewing of the *kohanim*'s clothing.

Like the *kohanim,* we have our special role in the service of *Hashem*. The clothes that we wear are like our uniform and when they are *tzanua* - fitting in style and covering properly - we have that added measure of *kedushah* that enables us to fulfill our roles.

CAN YOU THINK OF ANY OTHER CONNECTIONS BETWEEN THE KOHANIM'S CLOTHING AND TZNIUS?

There was a man from the town of Chelm who had been on the road all day and well into the night. Finally he arrived at an inn, exhausted. "Now, I can lie down and rest," he said to himself with relief.

But when he went to check in at the counter, the clerk shook his head apologetically.

"I'm sorry, sir. We have no room. We are completely full."

"Please," begged the traveler. "I am so tired and I cannot go on."

"I would be delighted to host you," explained the clerk. "But all our rooms are taken."

The man was distressed. "I don't need a room, just a bed. Perhaps you have a room with an empty bed."

Clearly, this traveler was not used to staying in hotels, the clerk thought to himself. But the fellow did look desperate and he felt sorry for him. "Look, I have an idea. Earlier this evening, an army officer checked in. He had his dinner and drank plenty of wine and barely made it back to his room. He's probably sound asleep for the night. There's an empty bed in his room...."

"Oh, please let me sleep there," the man begged, interrupting the clerk. "I'll go in very quietly. I won't make a sound, I promise. And if you wake me up before sunrise, I'll be sure to be gone before he gets up. He'll never know that I was there."

"Fair enough," said the clerk. The man thanked the clerk and paid for his lodgings. The clerk escorted his guest to the officer's room. "Just make sure you don't rouse him," he warned, "and leave as soon as I wake you." The traveler tiptoed in, lay down on the bed, and was soon fast asleep.

It was still dark outside when the clerk came in softly to wake him up. "Please hurry," he whispered as he closed the door gently. The traveler was true to his word. He rose quickly and quietly, silently groping around in the darkness in search of his clothes, which he had left on a chair. He dressed hurriedly, gathered his bags, and left the room. As he walked through the lobby on his way out, he glanced at his reflection in a mirror. Much to his surprise he saw that he was dressed as an army officer.

"Oh, my goodness," he exclaimed in displeasure. "That foolish clerk! Instead of waking me, a decent traveler from Chelm, he went and woke up the officer...."

Now, this could only have happened to a citizen of Chelm! But, there is some truth to be learned from that fellow. The clothes that we wear definitely make a statement about how we see and conduct ourselves.

Mrs. Klein, a school teacher who is also in charge of the drama club, says, "I always see a big difference in play practice and the final dress rehearsal, even if they are only one day apart. When the students are wearing their costumes, they act their parts better. Our actions in everyday life are also connected to the clothes we wear. And the way we dress can also make a difference in how others view us and expect us to act.

"Many of my students come from families that have not yet made a total commitment to *tznius*," Mrs. Klein relates. "One Sunday, a group of girls was riding the bus on their way to a park. I was sitting at the back and they did not see me. The bus was packed and only getting fuller as it rode down the avenue picking up passengers. At one stop, an elderly man got on looking around for an empty seat. Even though there were many girls on the bus, I noticed people glancing at Sarah, whose clothing was more *tzanua* than some of the others, expecting her to get up and offer him her seat. I don't think that anyone necessarily knew the girls personally, so they could have expected good manners from all of the girls. But it was clear that Sarah was singled out because of her modest appearance. Her clothing 'gave her away' as the one who should be the first to give up her seat, because a *tzanua* appearance is associated with good *midos*."

THE PEOPLE ON THE BUS JUDGED SARAH BY HER OUTER APPEARANCE. IF THIS WERE TO HAPPEN TO YOU, HOW WOULD IT MAKE YOU FEEL?
SHOULDN'T A PERSON'S MIDOS AND GOOD MANNERS COUNT MORE THAN OUTER APPEARANCES?

"The clothing I wear makes a statement to others, but it affects me as well," says Dena. "When I come home from school, I go straight to my room to change out of my school uniform and put on my regular clothes. I don't want to feel that I'm still in school. It's strange, because it's only outer clothing and the uniform is actually nice and comfortable. But changing into something else helps me unwind from school and feel more at home."

The following is a dress code from a well-known institution:

Head: Long hair should be tied back. No colored hair clips or combs. Discreet make-up. No overpowering perfume.

Hands: Short clean nails. Clear nail polish only.

Jewelry: No excessive jewelry. Only studs or small earrings. No charm bracelets or bangles.

Dress: Plain white blouse, preferably with collar and long or three quarter length sleeve. Black skirt, below knee level.

Shoes: All black sensible shoes. No sandals, boots, stilettos (excessively high heeled shoes) or slippers.

Does this sound like a high school dress code?

You might be surprised to find out that this sign was seen hanging in the personnel office of a prestigious non-Jewish hotel in Liverpool, England!

The managers of this hotel want their employees to make a good impression. They want their visitors to view them as dignified hosts who treat their guests with respect and efficiency. Their clothes help make this statement to others, and serve as a reminder for themselves. The business-like look says: "We are in this business and know how to do it well," and the modest look says: "We respect ourselves by wearing modest clothes that do not draw attention to our physical appearance but to the fact that we are here to serve you. You can be sure that we will respect you as well."

A GIRL WHO STRUGGLES TO LIVE UP TO TZNIUS STANDARDS SAYS: "DRESSING PROPERLY ON THE OUTSIDE WHEN THAT'S NOT WHERE I'M HOLDING ON THE INSIDE, MAKES ME FEEL LIKE A HYPOCRITE." DO YOU AGREE?

Did you notice that the hotel includes shoes on their list?

Some people might shrug and comment, "Come on! That's going too far!"

However, we see that the Torah hints that we need to pay attention to our shoes. In *Parashas Eikev*, the Torah describes the rewards for keeping *mitzvos*: וְהָיָה עֵקֶב תִּשְׁמְעוּן "And it will be as you will listen to my command" (*Devarim* 7:12). The word עֵקֶב which means "as you will" also means "heel." So we could say that even the heel has to "listen." In other words, even our shoes should conform to the Torah's guidelines for *tznius*. As styles change, we need to pay attention to the height and bulkiness of the heel.

The idea that our clothing plays an important part in the *tzanua* way of life goes back to the earliest times. Even the ancient Egyptians knew this. Potifar's wife was constantly thinking of ways to get Yosef *haTzaddik's* attention. She understood that she would be more successful in getting his attention if he would dress differently. The Torah tells us: וַתִּתְפְּשֵׂהוּ בְּבִגְדוֹ - "and she caught him by his garment" (*Bereishis* 39:12). Potifar's wife schemed, "I have to figure out how to get him to change his clothing. He dresses like a pious Hebrew. As long as he continues to dress like that, he will never pay any attention to me. Once I get him to dress like an Egyptian, he will be much more likely to respond to me" (*Zohar, Parashas Vayeishev* 238).

Yosef's mode of dress protected him in another way as well. Yosef knew the power of clothing, especially for a person in a position of power. After all, when he became the ruler, he mingled with all the top officials, not to mention Pharaoh himself! Dressing like an Egyptian would have certainly made his life easier. But he stood firm. He pictured his father's image in his mind and asked himself: Could I appear before my father, dressed in Egyptian fashion? Never!

Later, when the Jews were enslaved, Pharaoh decreed that the Jewish girls be brought up in the Egyptian culture. Even without his decree, this could easily have happened. The Jewish people had been living alongside the Egyptians for close to two hundred years! Yet Jewish women and girls kept their distance.

How were they able to accomplish this? Our Sages say: לֹא שִׁינּוּ אֶת לְבוּשָׁם - "they did not change their mode of dress" (*Bamidbar Rabbah* 13:17).

NOWADAYS, MANY TORAH JEWS DRESS SIMILARLY TO THE WAY NON-JEWS DO. SHOULD THINGS BE DIFFERENT?

After their marriage, Rabbi Sholom Ber and Rebbetzin Shterna Sarah Shneerson traveled to their new home. The carriage was laden with boxes and valises. His father, the Rebbe Maharash of Lubavitch, noticed that one of the boxes was oddly shaped.

"What is in that box?" he asked.

"It is a woman's hat," came the answer. "A gift for the bride."

The Rebbe asked to see the gift. He was handed an elegant hat whose style included a feather, as was worn by women at that time. He promptly removed the feather and returned the hat to the box.

Not all Egyptian clothing was necessarily immodest; some of the garments did indeed properly cover the person wearing them. Nevertheless, the Jewish women in Egypt did not buy their clothes from Egyptian tailors, even though they knew that some fashions might be in accordance with the length, fit and thickness of material that *tznius* requires. For they also knew that "the clothes make the man" and they did not want to be "made into" the likes of the Egyptians.

SHOULD WE NOT WEAR ANY OF THE STYLES THAT ARE WORN BY THE GENERAL PUBLIC?

WHEN I'M STRONG, I DON'T GO WRONG

From our ancestors in Egypt, leading right up to our modern times, the Jewish people have maintained the proper standard of tznius, disregarding what others may say. This takes strength and determination.

Leah is a person of such strength.

Leah says, "You know how some stores and businesses ask you to fill out a questionnaire about the quality of their merchandise and service? Well, when I go shopping I use my own questionnaire. As I browse through the aisles and find something that I like, the first thing I ask is: Does it cover properly? Then I ask: Is this really nice and appropriate for a tznius girl, or am I just another easy catch for the fashion designers in New York, France or Italy who are trying to convince me that this will make me feel 'in'? In the fitting room, I ask myself: Would I feel comfortable wearing this in front of an important person I look up to and respect?

"I like shopping this way. There is so much advertising all around trying to convince me to buy this, that, and the other. There are many girls dressing in certain ways that sometimes make me feel 'out of it' if I don't dress like that. So when I walk into a store with my own questionnaire, I feel like I am in control and have the choice to make up my own mind. That's when I really feel like a 'customer'; Jewish customs are what help me decide what to buy."

SOME OF US MAY NOT HAVE AS MUCH STRENGTH OF CHARACTER AS LEAH HAS. WHAT WOULD YOU SUGGEST AS ADDED INSURANCE TO PROPER SHOPPING?

"I try my best," sighs Rena. "I really look carefully. But it is so disappointing to spend hours and hours searching for clothes. The only payoff after having had nothing to eat all day, walking for hours in the mall and the continuous exercise of trying on clothes, is that you arrive home slightly thinner than when you left!"

Rena's mother adds, "This shopping business often leaves me in the cold. It's either too old, too bold, doesn't fit the mold, costs its weight in gold or is already sold."

Rena and her mother point out that it often takes a lot of physical energy to search for proper clothes. Perhaps even more than that, it takes a lot of inner strength. What is this inner strength? It is being determined and not giving in, for when we have been shopping for hours without success, we can be tempted to give in. We're simply too tired. Our eyes are too tired to check carefully; our hands are too tired to try on another shirt; our feet are too tired to carry us to yet another store; and our minds are just too tired to think. Yet, we must never shop without thinking.

We must think about who we are. The Torah recognizes that it takes willpower to live a life of *tznius*. In the song of praise that compliments the Jewish woman, Shlomoh *haMelech* states: עוֹז וְהָדָר לְבוּשָׁהּ - "She dresses in clothes of strength and glory" (*Mishlei* 31:25). Our Sages say (See *Zevachim* 116a): אֵין עוֹז אֶלָּא תוֹרָה - Strength lies in following the Torah way. They are telling us that we need to be strong and determined to do what is right. They are also telling us that living the Torah life will strengthen and protect us.

Tznius is singled out as uniquely bound to protection:

כִּי ה' אֱלֹקֶיךָ מִתְהַלֵּךְ בְּקֶרֶב מַחֲנֶךָ לְהַצִּילְךָ... וְלֹא יִרְאֶה בְךָ עֶרְוַת דָּבָר וְשָׁב מֵאַחֲרֶיךָ - For *Hashem*, your G-d, is found in the midst of your camp to save you...and there will not be a lack of

tznius among you, [for if so] He will withdraw Himself from you [and you will be unprotected]" (*Devarim* 23:15).

HOW WOULD YOU EXPLAIN THE CONNECTION BETWEEN TZNIUS AND PROTECTION?

The air out side was chilled, but inside, in the pounding hearts of the Jews of Germany, it felt icy. Numbness froze their ability to think straight and make the right decision. Many people sensed that on that night, the ninth of November 1938, later to be known as Kristallnacht, something was going to happen. But where? Which streets? Is it better to be downstairs or upstairs? Stick together or separate? These were the questions that were racing through the minds of many families. One family whose home bordered on the non-Jewish neighborhood decided to stay overnight with their relatives who lived in an area that they hoped would be safer.

"You go now," suggested Gitel, their teenage daughter. "I'll stay to hide things away, close all the shutters, and bolt the doors."

It was hard to be sure that this would be the best course of action, but her parents consented.

"Yes, we'll do that," they said. "It's better not to go out as a group. Please be careful and come quickly."

"I will," Gitel promised. "It's only mid-afternoon and it's quiet outside. There is still time till nightfall."

Gitel busied herself with the chores, hardly noticing the commotion that was building up outside. Suddenly, she heard loud cries followed by wicked laughter. Immediately she knew. Darkness had fallen for the Jews even though it was

not yet nighttime.

"What should I do?" she pondered. "I can't just walk down the street. Those German soldiers will spot me in a minute." She paced the floor, frantically trying to think of a plan. Suddenly, she caught sight of herself in the mirror and an idea came to her. She unbraided her long blond hair, messing it up to give it a carefree look and quickly put on dressy clothes. "I'll open the top button of my dress and I'll walk cheerily down the street as if I don't have a care in the world. Hopefully, they won't realize that I'm Jewish and they won't bother me."

But as Gitel descended the stairs, fumbling with the top button, she hesitated. She couldn't bring herself to open her top button. "I am a Jewish girl who has always led a life of tznius. I just can't do it." So with her button closed Gitel stepped out of the building and onto the street.

Nothing could have been more of a contradiction: Here she was, a young girl walking happy-go-lucky down the street looking about calmly, yet inside her heart was racing and her fists were clenched tight in her pocket.

Finally, she arrived at her relatives' house and fell crying into her mother's arms. All the pent up tension flowed freely with her tears. Between sobs, Gitel told her parents about her decision not to open her top button. Her mother gazed at her intently and gently drew out the short necklace that hung around Gitel's neck. She stroked her daughter lovingly and said, "You were so nervous, you must have forgotten you were wearing this necklace. I am proud of you, my daughter. Your strong commitment to tznius saved your life."

Hanging from her chain, hidden by the closed button, was a Jewish Star of David.

We are the people who are described as עַם קְשֵׁה עֹרֶף - a stubborn nation (*Shemos 32:9, et al.*) For over three thousand years we've been stubbornly sticking to the rules of the Torah. We will not break this chain of determination just because right now, for this particular moment, we are frustrated and tired of shopping. This is the glory of *tznius* - look at a *tzanua* person and you will see strength.

In *Shir HaShirim* (6:11) we read: אֶל גִּנַת אֱגוֹז יָרַדְתִּי - "I have gone down to an orchard of nut trees." This is speaking about *Hashem* Who has "gone down" to observe the Jewish people (Rashi). Why are they referred to as an orchard of nut trees? Our Sages explain that this is said in praise of the Jewish people. A nut that falls from the tree onto wet muddy ground can still be eaten because the outer shell protects its inner fruit. Jewish people who live a life of *tznius* can live among other cultures and not be affected by their non-*tznius* ideas and ways. *Tznius* is the solid shield that keeps our Jewishness strong, no matter what winds are blowing around us.

The Jewish people are also likened to a rose: כְּשׁוֹשַׁנָה בֵּין הַחוֹחִים כֵּן רַעְיָתִי בֵּין הַבָּנוֹת "Like a rose between the thorns, so is my beloved amongst other daughters" (*Shir HaShirim* 2:2). A rose is a beautiful flower with graceful and tender petals. It seems amazing that such a delicate flower grows so attractively surrounded by the prickly thorns of the rosebush. How is it that the sharp thorns don't tear the petals? If we look closer at the bush, we can see that the rose always grows above the thorny stems in such a way that the two have no contact. The rose stands apart from the branches and even a strong wind will not throw the flower against the thorns.

The Jewish people can live among other nations without being influenced by them in a harmful way. Like the rose that grows among the thorns while keeping a safe distance, a *tznius* way of life raises us above and away from "thorny issues" that can tear at the fabric of our life. As we hold our heads up with determination to keep our standards, we will blossom and flourish.

THE ROSE GROWS ABOVE THE THORNS BUT IT IS STILL CONNECTED TO THE SAME BRANCH. HOW CAN WE MAINTAIN THAT DELICATE BALANCE WITH OUR SURROUNDINGS?

"Oh no," groaned Faige. "My gray socks are in the wash and Henny's wearing the only burgundy pair we have."

"The sock drawer is filled to the brim," said her mother. "Take any other pair."

"But I wanted my socks to match the outfit I'm wearing," complained Faige.

"There are plenty of white pairs," her mother said patiently. "White goes with everything."

"I'm tired of white. I really wanted to wear something different today," insisted Faige.

Faige's grandmother, who was visiting, overheard the conversation. "Come here a moment, Faige'le. I'd like to share something with you that happened to me when I was about your age."

Faige went and sat down next to her grandmother. Everyone knew that Bubbie Goldstein grew up in the Warsaw Ghetto and lived through the horrors of World War II. But very few people knew much about her life, for she hardly ever spoke about her childhood. Whenever the children asked for stories, she would smile wistfully and say, "Come I'll play a game with you. Then you will have cheerful stories to tell your grandchildren about your old Bubbie who couldn't even beat you at a game of Torah cards."

And now Bubbie was actually offering to talk about her childhood.

"Life was very hard in the ghetto," she began. "I try not to think about those sad days, but your concern with matching socks brought back memories. You know, we didn't have any socks. Nor for that matter, anything decent that could pass for shoes, either. Not wearing proper shoes caused us much discomfort. But we would never have considered not having our legs covered properly. We knew that being a Jewish girl means to be tznius. The goyim never stopped for a moment to hate us and kill us just because we were Jewish. So how could we ignore who we were? So for lack of anything else, we ripped away the corners of the coarse, stiff material that covered the straw mattresses. From this rough fabric we made socks. They were prickly and uncomfortable, but we were tznius. The only thing that the faded, uneven stripes on those socks matched was the hardened lines on the wrinkled faces of the Jews in the ghetto."

It's not merely encouraging to know that we have this inner strength. We are commanded to put it to use. The Torah says: שֹׁפְטִים וְשֹׁטְרִים תִּתֶּן לְךָ בְּכָל שְׁעָרֶיךָ - "You shall appoint judges and policeman at all your gates" (*Devarim* 16:18). This *mitzvah* pertains to the safety of the city. The gates are the opening of a city. Judges are appointed to decide what is appropriate for the well-being and security of the city. But laying down rules is not enough. Someone has to make sure that those laws are kept. This is the job of the policemen. They have the power to enforce the law. Yet, the Torah is not only speaking about cities...

The Hebrew word שְׁעָרֶיךָ, "*your* gates," refers also to every individual. Just as the gates are the first part of the city we encounter as we approach, a person's appearance gives the first impression about him. This may seem a bit unfair. After all, we want people to look beyond our outer appearance. But not everyone does. And to be quite honest, many of us often judge others by first impressions and their outer looks. Knowing that this is human nature, the Torah reminds us not to overlook our appearance.

We are instructed to act as שֹׁפְטִים, to use proper judgment: to follow the guidelines of *tznius*, and decide what is appropriate for our appearance. Then the Torah tells us: Go ahead and act upon that judgment. You were commanded to appoint for yourselves "policemen." Your inner strength is like a policeman, making sure you are following those guidelines.

This is also the meaning of the royal title given to Jewish girls and women: בַּת מֶלֶךְ "daughter of a king." A king is in the position of the highest power. He makes sure that the law is enforced. As a daughter of a king, a Jewish girl has within her power the ability to ensure that she is living a life of *tznius*.

During the terrible rule of the Inquisition, the cruel church officials hunted the Jews with a hatred that knew no bounds. "We will get them!" they cried out to the cheering crowds. "We will force the Jews to convert to Christianity or die. Fellow citizens, join us in this holy act. Lead us to those stubborn Jews and we will reward you handsomely."

Many Jews were captured, tortured and burned to death. No one was safe, not even children. Among the unfortunate captives was a thirteen-year-old girl. The church officials assumed that such a young girl would not put up much resistance when faced with the possibility of being put to death. Thus, they were taken aback by her vehement reply: "No! Never! I will never abandon my faith and become a Christian."

Now, the inquisitors were accustomed to the Jews' refusals to abandon their faith, but none expected such conviction from a mere child. The girl's protest of strength and dignity enraged the officials even more than her belief.

"What insolence!" thundered the chief judge. "I will show her what becomes of those who disobey. She will die, but not by the stake. Tie her hair to a horse's tail and let him gallop around the city. This impudent girl will be dragged behind over rocks and thorns until she breathes no more."

The girl did not flinch at her terrible plight. One of the older officials was amazed at her courage. "How can this young girl be so brave and determined?" he wondered. He even felt sorry for her. He changed his tone and spoke to her kindly trying to convince her to save her life by agreeing to convert.

But the girl shook her head firmly. "I live as a Jew and I will die as a Jew. I am not afraid," she replied bravely. "But I do have one request."

A tense hush filled the room. Everyone leaned forward to hear what she would say.

"I have always lived a life of modesty and I wish to die modestly," the girl proclaimed. "As the horse drags me down the streets, my dress will lift up. I request that you attach my dress to my flesh with pins."

Mercilessly, the officers fulfilled her wish. Nothing but words of prayer was heard from the girl's mouth as she suffered her terrible plight.

Suddenly, she called out, "Stop! Stop!" The officers who accompanied the galloping horse thought that her spirit was finally broken. They were sure she was ready to convert. They were astonished to hear her say, "Some of the pins have fallen out. Put them back in so my dress will not lift up."

THREE CHEERS FOR HELPFUL PEERS

"When I read stories like that I am very moved," admits Chayah. "I get inspired and decide to do better, yet I still find it hard. You know how it is. You make a resolution to become more *tzanua* and along comes a friend and asks, "Since when have you become a *rebbetzin*?!""

Chayah is speaking about the age-old problem of peer-pressure.

When Avraham Avinu instructed Eliezer to search for a wife for Yitzchak, he said: לֹא תִקַּח אִשָּׁה לִבְנִי מִבְּנוֹת הַכְּנַעֲנִי אֲשֶׁר אָנֹכִי יוֹשֵׁב בְּקִרְבּוֹ - "Do not take a wife from the daughters of Canaan among whom I dwell" (*Bereishis* 24:3).

Why did Avraham mention that he lives among the people of Canaan? Obviously Eliezer knew where Avraham lived. What was Avraham trying to say by mentioning where he lived? What did that have to do with the mission that Eliezer was being sent on then?

The Chasam Sofer explains that Avraham was teaching Eliezer - and all of us - about peer-pressure. "If we lived somewhere else, I may have considered looking for a girl of fine character from the people of Canaan. She would enter our household and learn from our way of life. She would be far away from her previous friends and would be positively influenced by the environment in our home. But since we live here among the people of Canaan, it will be very hard for her to change. The girl would often meet up with old friends who may challenge her new way of life."

Avraham Avinu was aware of the negative effects of peer pressure. He did not rely even on the holy environment of his own household to overcome other influences.

Peer pressure could affect even the most righteous people.

The original name of Moshe Rabbeinu's attendant was הוֹשֵׁעַ, which means "to save." Before the *meraglim* left on their mission to spy out *Eretz Yisrael*, Moshe Rabbeinu added the letter י to Hoshea's name. The י stands for the name of *Hashem* (*Sotah* 34b, commenting on *Bamidbar* 13:16). The new name was now יְהוֹשֻׁעַ. Moshe prayed for him: "May *Hashem* save you from the advice of the *meraglim*." Moshe foresaw the sin of the *meraglim* and knew that Yehoshua needed that prayer. Even though Yehoshua was Moshe's closest disciple and could be trusted to do what was right, Moshe still prayed that he would not be influenced by the other *meraglim* as they were traveling together.

If Moshe was concerned about the challenge Yehoshua faced, how real is this concern for us! We know that others can persuade us even when we know that our way is right.

WHAT ARE YOUR SUGGESTIONS FOR DEALING WITH PEER PRESSURE?

Mrs. M. Greenberg is a busy mother of seven, the dean of a school, writes books, lectures, counsels and produces educational videos. But on Friday mornings she does what most Jewish homemakers do, cooks chicken and bakes kugel.

One Friday, elbow-deep in dough, she managed to answer the phone which would just not stop ringing. "It's probably important," she thought, "if they let it ring so many times."

"Hello," came a pleasant voice on the other end. "Are you Mrs. Greenberg? My name is Maya. I produce a T.V. program for Israeli Channel Two. We are doing a series on women's lifestyles. We thought it would be an attraction to feature observant women as well. Would you be willing to participate?"

Mrs. Greenberg was both surprised and amused. "I actually know a bit about filmmaking," she replied chuckling. "If you would like, you can come over right now and film a slice of life that is typical of an observant woman, zooming in on sticky dough and upright chicken legs."

"Good," thought Maya to herself. "She's observant and she has a sense of humor too." Speaking into the phone, she explained: "Let me explain, Mrs. Greenberg. We are inviting three other Orthodox women to the studio. Each one of you is accomplished in your respected fields, despite the fact that you are religious. You do not exemplify the typical observant woman who is confined to her private domain. You would be a real scoop for our talk show."

Now it was Mrs. Greenberg's turn to think to herself. "And I thought that these modern, well-educated career women would have dropped these outdated stereotypes long ago! I wonder if this is the right thing to do. On the one hand, it could be an opportunity to present a Torah message to the Israeli public. We work so hard to attract non-informed Jews to our outreach programs, and here is an enormously wide audience handed to us on a silver platter. On the other hand, I do not feel comfortable with this type of public setting."

Mrs. Greenberg resolved to speak to her Rabbi and asked Maya to call back in a few days. Upon the Rabbi's advice, Mrs. Greenberg participated public setting."

Mrs. Greenberg resolved to speak to her Rabbi and asked Maya to call back in a few days. Upon the Rabbi's advice, Mrs. Greenberg participated in the talk show.

On the following day, she had an appointment with the printer of the new book she had written. Ahuvah, the printer's secretary, greeted her with an exuberant smile. "I didn't know you were as good at the microphone as you are on paper," she exclaimed. Then she added: "You know, I am not observant. Many of the things you women said are foreign to me and I do not agree. But honestly, I wasn't listening to what you said as much as how you said it. You came across so dignified, confident and at peace with yourselves. And modest. Yes, modest. It was strange because in your circles, public exposure and especially of this type, would hardly be considered modest. Yet, that is precisely what you all appeared to be."

SENSITIVE AND AWARE – WE NEED TO CARE

As we learn what an important role *tznius* plays in our life and how other major issues are so directly connected to *tznius*, we are not surprised that our Rabbis, parents, and teachers speak about it constantly.

Avivah wonders if all this talk really helps. "Sometimes when people talk about a topic too much it actually produces the opposite response. We've been taught what the *halachah* is. How much more is there to say? When the topic of *tznius* comes up in class, I look around and see facial calisthenics! Eyes begin to roll, lower lips stretch downward, and heads move abruptly from side to side. Many girls just tune out."

If Avivah is right, why does everyone keep bringing up this topic?

When guests come over for Shabbos, you welcome them warmly at the door and invite them in with a smile. You show them to their room and offer them something to eat. You ask them if there is anything they need or if there is something else you can do for them.

All this attention clearly tells them that you are happy to host them and will do everything possible to make their stay pleasant. And yet, although you have already told your guests to feel at home, throughout Shabbos you ask them: "Would you like an extra pillow?" "Did you sleep well?" "Would you like a snack?" "Are the children disturbing you?" And your guest is urged: "Please take a second helping." "Have another slice of cake." "Please join us for a cup of tea." "Come read in the living room, the air conditioning is better there."

Even though we have clearly shown our guest that he is most welcome, our comments continuously give him the message that we are very happy he is with us and we care that he is comfortable. They also remind us to be more aware of our responsibility as hosts and to be sensitive to our guest's needs.

It works the same for *tznius*. Talking about *tznius* helps us become more aware. Since *tznius* is a way of life, it is a daily issue and the more sensitive and aware we are, the better we will become at living a life of *tznius*. So even when we are not following word for word what is being said, it is an opportunity for additional awareness.

If we do pay attention to what is being said, this awareness will work even better for us. Take Rochi, for example. She has this thing about homework. It somehow manages to get pushed off again and again. She has this nagging thought at the back of her mind that keeps coming up: "Homework, homework! I have to do my homework." Yet it doesn't get done.

Instead of just thinking "homework," Rochi might think of the points people were making; her teachers: "If you do your homework when you get home from school, and not late at night when you're tired, you would do a better job and get better grades"; her parents: "Do it now, then you'll feel relaxed and free from the constant nagging"; her sister: "Do it now, then you'll have a better chance that Mommy will agree to that sleepover party you want to have."

If Rochi would think about the different things people say about doing homework, her awareness of her responsibility to do it would grow. She wouldn't just groan and agree with that nagging thought at the back of her mind. She would think about the reasons and advantages, and instead of saying to herself, "Yes, I know I have to do it," she would say, "The things people say over and over really do make sense and are for my own good."

Many of the things we hear repeatedly about *tznius* do make a lot of sense. They also develop our sensitivity. The awareness that comes from constantly talking about the topic makes us much more sensitive to *tznius*.

CAN YOU THINK OF WAYS TO BRING UP THE TOPIC OF TZNIUS WITHOUT PROMPTING MOANS AND GROANS?

We truly do want to do what is proper and when we don't, it may be simply because we were not sensitive enough. When someone pointed out to Malkie that her top was too tight, she said, "I didn't wear this intentionally to look non-*tznius*, I just didn't notice that it must have shrunk in the wash." When someone commented to Nechamie that it was improper to sit crossed-legged on the curb while waiting for a bus, she responded, "I just wasn't thinking." When Shifi called out loudly in the street to her friends whom she hadn't seen all summer, she excused herself when her older sister shushed her; "Was I really shouting too loudly?"

Malkie, Nechamie, Shifi, and for that matter their friends, relatives, and all of the Jewish people really want to do the right thing.

Imagine you've just arrived at your cousin's wedding and you notice a stain on your clothes. You didn't notice it earlier when you were getting dressed, but under the bright lights of the wedding hall, it's impossible not to notice it.

Those bright lights are like the sensitivity sensors a person should develop to *tznius*. We should be able to notice for ourselves anything which needs to be corrected. Thus the constant talk about *tznius* will bring about awareness and awareness will bring about sensitivity, and hopefully we will no longer find ourselves in embarrassing situations where we have to excuse ourselves, saying, "Oh, I didn't realize...."

Once Rabbi Elchanan Wasserman, the renowned Rosh Yeshivah from Europe, came to America to raise funds for his yeshivah. He was being driven through Manhattan, riding in the back seat of a car that had shades on all its windows. As was his lifelong habit, Rabbi Wasserman was focused on his Gemara. All of a sudden his concentration was broken. He called out to the driver as if in distress, "Please drive through this street as quickly as you can!"

The driver, a native New Yorker, was taken by surprise. They were driving through an extremely non-tznius section of town, but from where he was sitting, engrossed in learning, Rabbi Wasserman couldn't possibly have seen the area. Obviously, it was his heightened sensitivity to *kedushah* that caused him to stir in extreme discomfort.

There is another positive result from talking about *tznius*. The words that we speak have a lot of power. When we say something, we are giving power to the idea that we are talking about and thus it becomes a real "thing." It's no coincidence that the Hebrew word for "talk," דִּבֵּר, shares the same letters as the word for "thing," דָּבָר.

There are many examples of how our words have an effect on reality, for instance: When we answer *amen* to a *brachah*: The *brachah* speaks of *Hashem*'s ruling over the world. When we say *amen* we are saying: "So be it, this is true." By saying that, we actually bring down more of *Hashem*'s influence into the world. When we wish a person who is not feeling well a *refuah sheleimah*: We are not just being polite. These well-wishes can actually hasten his recovery.

"You know, it's true what you're saying about words," agrees Tovah. "Last week we were planning our Purim party. Everyone was suggesting themes and the room was so full of fun ideas that it almost felt like we were having the party right then and there. We weren't doing anything but talking, but you could feel the energy in the air. Then, someone mentioned something negative about last year's party. It wasn't really about anyone, it was just a reminder about the flop we had last year. Suddenly the excitement fell flat. You could actually feel the atmosphere change. It took awhile to get back into the right mood."

Have you heard the phrase: "His words lingered in the air"? Tovah was probably referring to this idea. The words we say can contribute a lot to the setting we are in.

If talk about fun ideas helps create a fun atmosphere and negative words make the environment feel unpleasant, wouldn't talk about *tznius* help create a more *tzniusdik* surrounding?

There may be another way of looking at the need to speak about *tznius* constantly and directly. There is something about *tznius* that has made it one of the most difficult challenges of our day. Many Rabbis and leaders have pointed out that this is the main *yetzer hara* of our times. Perhaps we can understand this by taking a glance at the *yetzer hara* of ancient times - idol worship.

The Torah repeats the commandment not to worship idols many times, for example: וַתִּרְאוּ אֶת שִׁקּוּצֵיהֶם וְאֵת גִּלֻּלֵיהֶם וכו' - "And you will see their repulsive and revolting idols...Beware not to be drawn to serve them" (*Devarim* 29:16). Yet, if the idol worship is so disgusting, why would the Torah have to warn people not to be drawn to it to serve it?

The pull of our environment is very strong and the sights that we see can make a firm impression upon us. A person can see things that may not appeal to him at all, yet seeing these things can affect him and he might be drawn in. This explains why the Torah states this warning and repeatedly mentions the commandment of not worshiping idols.

I'M NOT LAX,
WHEN I RELAX

As our sensitivity to *tznius* deepens, it becomes part of who we are. It is constantly on our minds and in our hearts. At home, in school, at shul or elsewhere we are careful to appear "good." Yet what about other places? On a trip, at camp, in the park, in all those places where we relax and take it easy. Are we "good" there too? The Torah says we should be.

Words of praise for this are so meaningful that every day we begin our *tefillah* with them: מַה טֹּבוּ אֹהָלֶיךָ יַעֲקֹב מִשְׁכְּנֹתֶיךָ יִשְׂרָאֵל - "How good are your tents, Yaakov, your dwelling places, Yisrael." A tent is a temporary dwelling. Yet even there, away from our regular place of living, our appearance must be proper and "good" - we shouldn't compromise our standards of *tznius*.

We are reminded of this every *Shabbos Mevarchim*, when we say a special *tefillah*, asking for good things to come in the new month: וַתִּתֶּן לָנוּ...חַיִּים שֶׁל חִלּוּץ עֲצָמוֹת חַיִּים שֶׁיֵּשׁ בָּהֶם יִרְאַת שָׁמַיִם וְיִרְאַת חֵטְא - "Grant us...a life of unrestrained physical activity, a life of fear of heaven and fear of sin." Among other things, we are asking *Hashem* to bless us so we may feel relaxed and not stressed. Yet, directly after that, we pray that we may have more *yiras Shamayim* and fear of sin.

Why do these requests follow each other? Relaxation is one thing and *yiras Shamayim* is another! Yet we know that when we are looking for relaxation, we might fall short of the standards of *tznius*. We may pay more attention to how our clothes, our looks, and our activities serve our need to relax, than how appropriate they are in our *avodas Hashem*.

"Of all places in the world," relates Tzippy, "Massada, the Second-Temple fortress in the Judean desert, was the last place I thought I would be jolted by a strong message of sensitivity to tznius.

"I come from a very observant family and all through my high school years, tznius was always presented as much more than covering elbows and knees. Everyone always stressed the overall 'look.' This made a lot of sense to me and I thought my friends and I had developed the appropriate sensitivity.

"After I graduated, I went to seminary in Israel. Just before our winter break our school took a trip to Massada, and we were guided to the top of the majestic mountain, stopping at various sites. One of our stops was a walled-in area, lined with stone benches along the walls, which our guide told us was a synagogue.

"Our group was entering the site when another tour group arrived. As I had experienced time and again in Israel, people are friendly and inquisitive and love to play 'Jewish geography'. They always asked where we were from, which school we go to, and where else we would be touring that day. This group was French, so the person asking the questions was their

Israeli guide. When we told him the name of our seminary, he knotted his forehead, and said that he'd never heard of it. 'Is it a chareidi (ultra-Orthodox) school?' he asked.

"I cringed. My friends and I all come from yeshivish Orthodox families, and we all had a proper Torah upbringing. I would have thought it would be obvious that we were very religious, or as the Israelis say, 'chareidi.' I looked around and sadly concluded that it wasn't so obvious. Some of us had chosen to overlook the 'look' and justified the very casual wear as okay for a field trip."

Our *tznius* makes a difference - in how other people perceive us and how we are perceived by *Hashem*. The words mentioned earlier are taken from the *Shabbos Mevarchim tefillah*. Yet even before we approach *Hashem* in prayer, *tznius* plays an important role. *Hashem* wants to hear our *tefillos*. Yet we need to remember that He is looking at us as well as listening to us. Actually, Shlomoh *haMelech* says that He "looks" before He "listens," as it is written: הַרְאִינִי אֶת מַרְאַיִךְ הַשְׁמִיעִנִי אֶת קוֹלֵךְ - "Show me your appearance...let me hear your voice" (*Shir HaShirim* 2:14). Our Sages explain that this teaches us to make sure we have the proper appearance when standing before *Hashem*. The *pasuk* mentions appearance first and prayer afterwards. Surely after *Hashem* sees our dedication to *tznius*, He will listen to our *tefillos*.

TEFILLAH IS CALLED, עֲבוֹדָה שֶׁבַּלֵּב
SERVICE OF THE HEART. SO WHY DOES OUR
OUTER APPEARANCE MAKE A DIFFERENCE?

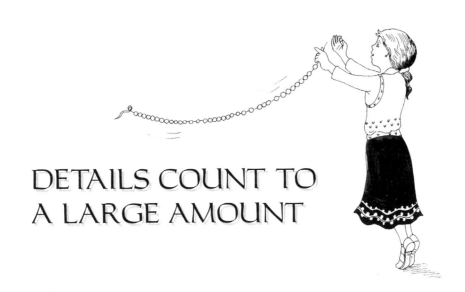

DETAILS COUNT TO A LARGE AMOUNT

"Okay," says Estie. "I get the idea. *Tznius* is a major focus and we need to be sensitive and aware. Clothes *do* reflect the person wearing them. But what really gets me is the nitty-gritty. If *tznius* is such a lofty way of life, why boil it down to so many details? I'm constantly hearing:

'Is that a knee I see or is the latest rage beige?'
'Is the blouse too frilly or does it look plain silly?'
'Is that one too many a bangle and do those earrings dangle?'
'It seems unclear if the sock's too sheer, or maybe it's just worn out from last year.'

Isn't the point to have a *tznius* look? Why get so particular?"

Perhaps we can help Estie and others view the attention that is paid to details in a more positive light. In the Torah we do not find many details about *tznius*. As with other *mitzvos*, our Sages and Rabbis set down the details and guidelines. Our Rabbis comment that it is actually a compliment to Jewish women and girls that the Torah does not go into great detail on matters of *tznius*, for it shows that *Hashem* puts His trust in Jewish women and girls. They have a natural feeling for *tznius* and will even go beyond the *halachah* in expressing how much they value and treasure this way of life.

Certainly we should strive to be worthy of the confidence *Hashem* has in us. We should view the detailed guidelines not as a burden, but rather as an aide to help us to live up to that trust.

A house full of mourners;
People came and went,
Huddling in corners
Many hours were spent.

Memories were shared
And stories were told
By people who cared-
They were young and old.

For who did not know
The Klausenberger Rebbe?
It was time for him to go,
Yet we were not ready.

This giant of a man
Who lost in the war
All that a father can -
His family was no more.

Eleven children and his wife
They took away,
But he insisted on life
And taught others the way.

From the ashes of fire
He uplifted people's hearts,
Assisting without tire
To help them restart.

And now he was gone
People came to mourn,
Telling how his light shone
And how survivors were reborn.

Among them was a woman
Clutching a small bag,
As if it were human
But you could see it was a rag.

The woman held it high,
As the others looked in shock,
Dangling by their eyes
Was an old worn-out sock.

Another sock followed,
And people continued to stare;
The woman's voice was hollow
She said: "It's the Rebbe's pair.

"One cold dreary day,
It was chilly and damp,
I was making my way
In the survivors' camp.

"The Rebbe caught sight
And called me aside:
'My daughter, our plight...
I know you have tried,

"'But legs that are bare -
It is not our way.'
And I just stood there
Too embarrassed to say

"But the Rebbe, he knew
That I just didn't have,
So he took off his shoe
That was torn right in half.

"The socks in his hand
With fatherly love
He said: 'It's the command
Of Hashem up above

"'It's your obligation
Much more than mine;
Teach the next generation
To be tznius and fine!'"

In *Halachah,* we find details that safeguard the *mitzvoz.* These details are called *gezeiros,* which means "decrees." These rules are intended to create the right setting for the *mitzvah.*

Let's think about Shabbos. In addition to the Torah's "letter of the law," our Rabbis have given us additional guidelines. Many of them have to do with very detailed activities, like cooling hot water by using two cups when making tea or not touching a pencil. These details enable the atmosphere to be *Shabbosdik.* We are not just concerned with a check-off list of *halachos* so we can pat ourselves on the shoulders and say: "Good for me, I did everything I was supposed to." A person can follow the strict *Halachah* and still be missing out on the whole Shabbos experience.

Imagine Shabbos without the *gezeiros* and guidelines our Rabbis have instructed: People could get up in the morning and dress in their weekday clothes. They could switch on lights with their elbows or ask a non-Jew to do it. They could handle money and carry it around in an unusual way, like stuffing it into the lining of a hat.

A woman could cook meals by switching on the cooker with a pinky or by asking the non-Jewish household help to do it. She could even wash the dishes in the dishwasher if she turned it on in an unusual way. This description can go on and on until you would hardly recognize the day as Shabbos! We could still be keeping the laws of Shabbos but we would lose the whole atmosphere which is very much a part of the uniqueness of Shabbos.

The same can apply to many *mitzvos*, and even more so to *tznius*. Because *tznius* is a way of life, the way we keep it - the spirit of this *mitzvah* - really makes a difference. All the attention paid to the details contribute to the total picture of a *tzanua* person - the type of person *Hashem* commands and trusts us to be.

Paying attention to details also says a lot about our relationship with *Hashem*. When wrapping a birthday present for a good friend we pay attention to every detail: the color of the wrapping paper, the card and envelope, the ribbon and a matching bow. Our friend notices that we have considered these details, and realizes how much we care. When we keep *mitzvos* with care and attention to details we show *Hashem* how much we treasure our relationship with Him.

We should also think about other *mitzvos,* which have many details that we consider very seriously and do not overlook. Like *kashrus*, for example. We are very careful to check and inquire about the ingredients of every product. Before we walk into a restaurant, we check to see that there is a reliable *hechsher*, not relying just on somebody's word. If there's the slightest doubt about the *kashrus* of a certain product, we don't touch it. We don't say that we know other people who eat it. We don't question why we shouldn't eat it. We don't ask if the concern we have about this food is written clearly in the Torah or if is it something our Rabbis have instructed us to do. We don't think twice about not eating it - we simply just don't do it!

"It's true," admits Estie. "I don't argue with my mother or teachers when it comes to kashrus, and I can see the truth in having the same attitude towards *tznius*."

We must be particular in following these guidelines because, like Estie, some people think that overlooking something that is only a "small" detail is okay. But missing a "small" detail can gradually lead to a serious decline in *tznius*. We are reminded of this from the people whose culture was the foundation for our modern times - the Greeks.

The ancient Greeks led a lifestyle that was the exact opposite of *tznius*. They were obsessed with physical beauty and perfecting their bodies, drawing attention away from the true essence of a person - that which is within . The Hebrew word for their country, Greece, is יון. Take a close look at these three letters. The י starts off very small; the next letter, the ו, looks like a long י, and the third letter ן looks like an elongated ו. A person can start with ignoring a "small" detail, but this often leads to continuously sliding down and lowering the standard of *tznius*.

SHAINDY CLAIMS THAT SHE KNOWS HER LIMITS: "JUST BECAUSE I MAY OVERLOOK A SMALL DETAIL, I KNOW I WILL NOT GO FURTHER." WHAT DO YOU THINK?

Another way of understanding the attention that is paid to the detail of *tznius*, is by taking an honest look at looks...

"I think I know what that means," suggests Avigail. "Someone can be dressed or be acting in such a way that I think to myself, 'I can't say that it's not *tznius*, but I can't say that it is *tznius* either.'"

Avigail is pointing out one of the aspects of *tznius* that creates the need for guidelines in the details. The opposite of *tznius* is *pritzus*. This is a harsh word that paints a picture of someone who may be called shameless, coarse or bad-mannered - in other words, the total opposite of anyone who is *aidel*, proper and modest. Because they are so different, people may consider a certain look or behavior acceptable, saying, "This is certainly not *pritzus,* so why shouldn't I wear or do it?"

But not everything that is not *pritzus* should automatically be considered *tznius*. The space between the two is often called the "gray" area. Many activities, accessories, and clothing fall into the "gray" area. But we are not left to wander about clueless in this uncertain zone. We have direction. Our Sages and Rabbis have considered this "gray" area and have gone into great detail to provide us with clear guidelines. Our own *tznius* sensitivity and awareness, heightened by the attention paid to details, enables us to make proper decisions in these "gray" areas.

LIST TYPES OF ACTIVITIES, CLOTHING, ACCESSORIES OR BEHAVIOR THAT MAY FALL IN THE "GRAY" AREA.

Indeed, *Hashem* looks very favorably at us when we make an effort at a time of doubt. Going back to the example of Shabbos, we sing in one of the Shabbos *zemiros*: הַמְאַחֲרִים לָצֵאת מִן הַשַּׁבָּת וּמְמַהֲרִים לָבוֹא - "Who delay when departing from the Shabbos and hurry to enter." This song praises people who introduce Shabbos early, before the required time, and extend it past *Havdalah* time. Why are they praised? It is not merely because this shows how grateful they are for having Shabbos. The song praises those people who make an effort to ensure that there is no *doubt* about their keeping Shabbos in its proper time - for here on earth there may be some doubt or disagreement as to when exactly Shabbos begins and ends.

In truth, though, the beginning and end of Shabbos is a matter of exact timing. In our prayers we say: וּמַעֲבִיר יוֹם וּמֵבִיא לַיְלָה ה' צְבָאוֹת שְׁמוֹ - "He causes the day to pass and brings on the night...G-d Almighty is His name." Only *Hashem* Himself knows exactly when day ends and night begins. So by bringing in Shabbos earlier and ending it later, a Jew shows that he is being very careful at a time of doubt, demonstrating how he values his relationship with *Hashem*. *Hashem* appreciates this and we sing words in praise of this.

We should have the same attitude towards *tznius*. *Hashem* looks very positively upon the person who takes extra measures and makes an effort to be free of doubt. In striving to live a life of *tznius* there are so many opportunities to go beyond the level of doubt, and by doing so we will arouse *Hashem*'s mercy and earn merit for ourselves.

The Rebbe of Munkatch wrote the following story, which he witnessed in his childhood.

The Beis Din of Hoklive, Hungary, was summoned with urgency. The government had issued an order to clear away part of the Jewish cemetery to make way for a new railroad. This meant relocating many of the graves, some of which were hundreds of years old. The task had to be done in accordance with Halachah and with proper respect for the deceased's remains. Many rabbis and learned elders set out for the cemetery accompanied by curious townsfolk for whom this was a rare event.

In the midst of the work, there was a sudden commotion around one grave. Everyone crowded around to see what it was all about. The grave was over a hundred years old, yet the body being exhumed was whole and unaffected, as if it had just been buried.

"This person must certainly have been one of the thirty-six hidden tzaddikim in his generation to have merited this," someone murmured in awe.

But as they peered closer to the ancient writing on the tombstone, they were astonished to read that this was a woman who was praised for her extreme dedication to a life of tznius.

Such dedication to *tznius* is due to ongoing sensitivity, which helps us make the right decision in times of doubt. When we develop a heightened sensitivity, we can begin to appreciate higher standards of *tznius* such as those of the exceptional woman Kimchis, as related in the Talmud.

Kimchis lived in the time of the second *Beis haMikdash;* she merited to see each of her seven sons serve as *kohanim gedolim*. When the Sages asked what she did to merit such children, she replied, "The beams of my house have never seen the hairs of my head" (*Vayikra Rabbah* 20:7).

Upon hearing her reply the Sages said:

כָּל קִמְחַיָּיא קֶמַח וְקֶמַח דְּקִמְחִית סֹלֶת - "The flour of most people is *kemach,* a mixture of coarse and fine flour, but the flour of Kimchis is *soles*, fine flour" (*Ibid.*).

Our Sages praised her with a play on the root of her name - Kimchis/*kemach.* What were our Sages saying?

They were praising her *tznius*, comparing the effort she made to other women. Others were in the category of *kemach.* In order to obtain flour that is good enough to bake with, you need to put it through a sifter. After the sifting it can be used, yet it will still have some coarseness to it.

But Kimchis is compared to *soles*, for in order to get this smooth, more delicate flour you have to sift it through a very fine sieve.

Some people's idea of being *tznius* is to "sift" their appearance and behavior through what they think is an acceptable "sieve." This means that they have checked that there is no obvious *pritzus.* Anything that is improper is not part of their wardrobe or actions. But as we said before: non-*pritzus* is not automatically total *tznius*.

Let's take an example from daily life. We all know that it is very important to be kind and there are many people who are careful not to hurt others. Imagine that you have a new girl in your school. Being a perceptive person, you notice several things about her. First of all, whenever she speaks to the other girls, she tries not to use words which will offend anyone. In trying to get others to do what she wants, she does not demand. And she helps others when she is asked.

This girl sounds like a decent person, but would you consider her to be a *kind* person? Indeed, all she is doing is making sure she is not being unkind! A truly kind person is someone who constantly goes out of her way to be kind, searching for opportunities to show kindness.

We can say the same for *tznius*. It's definitely good to make sure that our appearance and actions are not *pritzus*. But *tznius* is much more than that. It is having an ongoing awareness, putting in effort and genuinely feeling positive about the image that *Hashem* wants us to present.

This was the attitude in Kimchis that our Sages were praising. Kimchis was not satisfied with regular flour. She wanted to make sure she was doing more than just do away with the coarse bran of the grain. She strived for finer flour. She went out of her way even in areas that others may overlook. Even in the privacy of her own home she was most careful. She knew that *tznius,* more than just doing away with what's improper, is a way of life where we actively make every effort to do what is proper.

WE ARE TAUGHT TO LEARN FROM EXAMPLE. DO WOMEN LIKE KIMCHIS SEEM TOO LOFTY FOR US TO EMULATE?

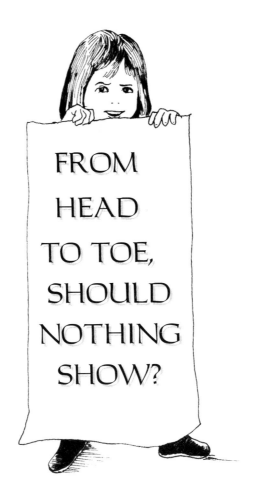

FROM HEAD TO TOE, SHOULD NOTHING SHOW?

"When I hear stories about people from the ancient times," says Yehudis, "I sometimes think to myself: Okay, they set the example for us, so let's be like them. Let's go the whole nine yards, literally! Let's take nine yards of material or however much it takes and wrap it around us from head to toe in full tunic style. Some religions still require clothes like that. And some even cover their face with a veil and their hands with gloves. Let's do that and we'll be the utmost in *tznius*."

Yehudis is suggesting to go back in time, but in response to her it would be wise to go back to basics. What is behind all this covering of the body? Is our body so negative that it has to be covered?

Quite the opposite. גוּף יִשְׂרָאֵל קָדוֹשׁ הוּא - "The physical body of Israel is holy." Holy

means separate, set aside, and given its specific space and respect.

Our Sages tell us that *Hashem* appreciates the Jewish people for safekeeping this holiness by their *tzniusdik* behavior and dress. We see this when the Torah counts the people and lists the names of their families, for example: לְחֶצְרֹן מִשְׁפַּחַת הַחֶצְרוֹנִי - "Of Chetzron, the Chetzroni family" (*Bamidbar* 26:6). *Hashem* takes the letters of His name, י and ה, and adds it to the name of the family - ה at the beginning and י at the end - because of the *tznius* way that the families lived.

There are many precious, important or expensive things in our home which we treat with special care. Fine furniture is protected with plastic or cloth. Expensive jewelry is hidden in a safe. Old family pictures are kept in a drawer separate from other albums.

One of the ways in which we regard those things that are holy to us is to cover them. Holiness is special, and constant display would detract from its specialness. A Torah scroll is holy - it is draped in a mantle. A *mezuzah* is holy - it is placed inside a cover. The parchments of *tefillin*, which contain *pesukim* from the Torah, are inside leather compartments. Even in the holiest place on earth in the *Beis haMikdash,* the same rule applies. In the *Kodesh haKodashim* stood the אֲרוֹן, in which the לֻחֹת הַבְּרִית were kept. Because the אֲרוֹן contained the holy לֻחֹת, it was covered with the כַּפֹּרֶת, a finely pounded gold sheet placed on top.

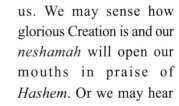

That which is holy, we cover. The body of a Jew is holy, so we cover it. Why? Because it contains *kedushah.*

What is this holiness inside of us that even makes our body holy?

It is our *neshamah*, that part of *Hashem* Himself which He gave each one of us. Our bodies are holy, because they house our *neshamah.* So our real self is actually our *neshamah,* which is, as we said, a part of *Hashem. Hashem* wants to fill this world with His holiness. So we need to express our *neshamah* and reveal it, in order to fill this world with *Hashem*'s holiness.

How do we do express ourselves?

With our eyes and ears we can see sights and hear sounds all around us. We may sense how glorious Creation is and our *neshamah* will open our mouths in praise of *Hashem.* Or we may hear

of a person in need and our *neshamah* will cause the look in our eyes and the words in our mouth to tell that person that we care. These are only a few of the many ways that we express ourselves.

We mentioned our eyes, ears, and mouth. What do they all have in common? They are all part of our face. The word for face in Hebrew is פָּנִים, *panim*. This is the same word as פְּנִים, *pnim*, which means: the inside. It is no coincidence that these words use the same letters, because we express what is inside of us, our *pnim*, through the different parts of our face, our *panim*.

We also use our hands to express ours פְּנִימִיּוּת. We can stroke, hold or hug when our *neshamah* wants to show care. We can write, paint or sculpt when our *neshamah* wants to express creativity. We can cook or bake when our *neshamah* wants to nurture.

But can my lower thigh express the real I?
Can my left knee show the inner me?
Does my right arm bring out my inner charm?
And do any of my toes tell what my *neshamah* knows?

Now, we can go back to Yehudis's suggestion and see that "going the whole nine yards" is not the ultimate in *tznius*. *Tznius*, as the Jewish way of life, requires that we cover our bodies, which are holy, but we do not cover those parts of us which enable us to reveal our *neshamah*. This is the message in *Tehillim* (45:14): כָּל כְּבוּדָה בַת מֶלֶךְ פְּנִימָה - "The glory of a king's daughter is her inner real self."

As we choose the clothes which cover us, we recall those holy objects - a Torah scroll, a *mezuzah* and the *aron* that are covered. They are not merely draped or wrapped. Their covering is dignified as befits their contents. Our clothes should be respectable as befitting our *neshamah*, which is our real self. It is quite clear that the oversized, baggy, or 'I don't care what I look like' styles, as well as unkempt clothing, would be an inappropriate covering for our bodies, which contain our *neshamah*.

This is especially important regarding our Shabbos wear. On Shabbos, the day itself is holy, and we receive an additional *neshamah*. We should insist on dignified and proper clothing. In *Megillas Esther*, we read that Mordechai sat in front of the king's gate donned in sackcloth. Esther sent a messenger with a change of clothing, "for one is not to enter the gates of the king's palace dressed in sackcloth" (*Esther* 4:2). This *pasuk* can refer to the King of kings, *Hashem* (*Sefer HaChinuch, mitzvah* 149). And this holy day which *Hashem* commands us to honor is called the Shabbos queen. It is disrespectful to 'dress down' on Shabbos. Quite the contrary, our Shabbos wardrobe should be respectable and in honor of this holy day.

IF A GIRL WOULD CHOOSE TO "COVER IT ALL," WOULD YOU THINK IT RIGHT TO DISSUADE HER?

Many people flocked to the Rebbe's courtyard - rabbis, Chassidim, guests, and even a hoard of matchmakers with suggestions for a suitable wife for the Rebbe's son. Among the callers was a poor widow. She had come to ask for a blessing. "I am not asking for myself," she claimed. "I have come on behalf of my daughter. She is a very fine girl with many virtues and I beseech the Rebbe to give her a blessing for a good shidduch."

To the woman's surprise, instead of responding with a blessing, the Rebbe asked, "Many virtues? What are they?"

Obligingly, the woman listed her daughter's fine qualities.

"Is that all?" the Rebbe inquired. "Is there anything else worthy of mentioning?"

By this time the woman was quite embarrassed - but the Rebbe was asking. She overcame her discomfort and related, "I hadn't intended to share this, but as the Rebbe is inquiring about deeper qualities, I will tell.

"In our neighborhood it's become the habit of girls to gather on Shabbos afternoon. They stroll together picking up each other at their houses. I noticed that my daughter does not join her friends and asked her why. She gently avoided an answer. After numerous times, she finally said that she would prefer to keep her reason to herself. But I insisted that she tell me, and she reluctantly explained. 'At the time that the girls go out on Shabbos afternoon, the streets are crowded with boys and men making their way to the shul and yeshivah. I don't think it's tzniusdik to be out at that time.'"

Upon hearing this, the Rebbe stood up obviously moved. "Blessed be Hashem Who has brought to me the girl who is suitable to be the wife of my righteous son. I am proud to have this girl, whose inner voice of tznius speaks louder than her surroundings, as my daughter-in-law."

The girl's mother could not decide if she was more amazed than happy. Soon, the couple became engaged, amidst much joy. At the festivities the Rebbe declared: " כָּל כְּבוּדָה בַת מֶלֶךְ פְּנִימָה (Tehillim 45:14). A girl whose glory is inward, is obviously a daughter of a king. Who would pass up the opportunity to marry into the king's family?!"

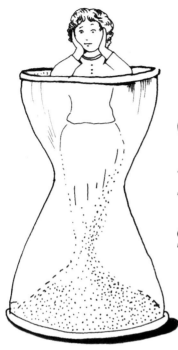

CAN'T IT WAIT AWHILE, THIS TZNIUS STYLE?

"You know," says Henny, "all these ideas are nice. However, it would even be nicer if they were easy to remember and make part of our everyday thoughts. I think my friends and I are working on ourselves to be *tzanua*. Every person has a different pace - it takes time. Why don't people just leave us alone in the meantime and let us work things out? We'll get there eventually."

Henny may not be aware of what can be going on, "in the meantime." If we keep the guidelines of *tznius*, even when we haven't yet internalized it all, it will have an effect not only on our own selves but also on others, as well as on the level of *kedushah* in the world.

Living a life of Torah and *mitzvos* requires that we have קַבָּלַת עוֹל מַלְכוּת שָׁמַיִם that we take upon ourselves to accept *Hashem*'s will. In the beginning of this book, we described modesty as being humble, respectful and *aidel*. These *midos* are the building blocks of a life of קַבָּלַת עוֹל. As we practice *tznius*, we are molding within ourselves the nature of a Jew who can accept *Hashem*'s will with ease and joy.

As explained above, *tznius* is the way we draw attention to our *real* self. When other people meet us, even without saying a word, we are challenging them to also pay more attention to their inner self, their *neshamah.* Have you heard the saying: "A picture is worth a thousand words"? We can spend so much time trying to convince others that they should express their *neshamah,* yet meeting people who are doing just that can be so much more impressive.

Yehudis Lipkin is an active member in the women's committee of the vibrant Jewish community in Miami. She is a mother of nine children, eight of them girls!

She says: "One can never underestimate the long-term effect a person who dresses tzniusdik, can have on others. The first girls I ever encountered who were dressed in the tznius way, didn't know that their mode of dress affected me. And though I hadn't a clue about tznius, their appearance changed my life. Strange as it may sound, I became committed to tznius long before I knew anything about being Jewish!"

Recalling her own journey to Yiddishkeit, she says, "In raising my own daughters, I see that tznius can be a challenge for anyone, and for someone like me - a then nine-year-old daughter of a fashion designer, living on the beachfront - you'd think it should have been a real test. Yet, for me personally, it wasn't.

"You see, back then, I was Judy Kramer, a happy-go-lucky youngster growing up with the Florida sun, beach and water sports. Not exactly the epitome of tznius as you can imagine. Then, my picture perfect lifestyle shattered along with my left arm and leg in a terrible car accident. Thank G-d, the doctors were able to 'put me back together again', but I was left with scars that made me want to stay inside and hide away for life.

"My mother, a creative fashion designer, custom made ingenious patterns to hide the scars, but I always felt uncomfortable among my classmates and friends with their skimpy outfits. Nothing my parents said could ease my discomfort. I felt that everybody was always staring at my scars.

"One day, I was with my mother shopping at the supermarket. As we stood in line at the checkout counter, I noticed a woman pushing a loaded cart accompanied by two girls. They caught my attention because they were dressed so differently from the usual Miami wear. I had never seen young girls dressed in what I learned later to be the tznius way. They were wearing similar outfits and one of them looked my age.

"I don't know what possessed me at that moment, but I walked over to them. Maybe it was the constant nagging inside of me because of my scars. 'Hi' I said. 'I'm Judy. Are those your school uniforms? Which school do you go to?' All I could think was - I would like to go to school where the uniform would hide everything.

"In frank southern friendliness the girls told me which school they went to and responded that they were not wearing uniforms but that this is the way they dressed after school hours as well. My heart skipped a beat and my mind raced with plans. I politely concluded the conversation and went right to my mother. 'I want to change schools,' I said adamantly, as only a stubborn and pained nine-year-old can.

"There were many reasons for my parents to reject the idea: It was an orthodox school and we weren't even members of a reform synagogue (I could barely pronounce the Hebrew name of that school properly); it was mid-year; the school was far; and I didn't know anybody who went there. But I didn't care. The only thing that mattered was that I would wear clothes that would hide my scars and I wouldn't feel out of place.

"In their desperate desire to ease my plight, my parents consented. Along with the change of schools came a progressive change in our family's lifestyle. As eager as I was to dress my body, I discovered that I needed to address my neshamah as well. All I cared about initially was to cover up, but I discovered that I needed to uncover my real self. Those two girls, who became my best friends, brought me to Yiddishkeit through their tznius; yet they had no idea at the time that it was because of their tznius that an innocent 'chance' encounter affected the lives of other Jews."

Everyone agrees that the environment we live in is greatly lacking in *tznius*. Many people are looking for some magic formula that will somehow purify our surroundings. We can help. Our environment includes you and me, your friends and mine, our homes and our streets. In our homes we can make a difference. The Torah calls women and girls בֵּית יַעֲקֹב, "the house of Yaakov" (*Shemos* 19:3). This teaches us that we are the ones who create the atmosphere in our homes.

Rabbi Yitzchok Hutner told the following story:

One day, when I was about ten years old, I came home from cheder and announced happily, "Today I have finished learning the entire *Mishnah* of *Bava Kama!*" My mother looked at me with a radiant smile.

"Is that so?" she exclaimed in delight. She immediately went to the dining room, took out an elegant white tablecloth and some decorative candles and laid them out on our Shabbos table. She then went into her bedroom and returned a short time later wearing the new dress that my father had bought for her for the upcoming *Yom Tov*.

"I am wearing this dress today," she said, "because the day my son finishes learning a tractate of the *Mishnah*, is a *Yom Tov* for me."

Rabbi Hutner's mother taught us how a woman can use her fine clothing to create an environment in her home. Her dressing up says: Completing a portion of Torah study is a good reason for festivity and elegant dress.

IT'S NOT JUST ME
THAT PEOPLE SEE

Since we are also part of the environment, when we practice *tznius* outside, we are cleansing the air by bringing more *kedushah* into the world. The environment then changes for the better, even if it only means our little space has improved.

However, our personal space is really not all that personal. In *Tehillim* (144:12) David *haMelech* compares Jewish daughters to the corner bricks of a wall: בְּנוֹתֵינוּ כְזָוִיֹת - "our daughters are like cornerstones." *Malbim* explains: When a wall is being constructed, the corners are built first. The bricklayers then draw a string from one corner to the other to make sure that the central bricks are set at the right height. In this way, the corner bricks are the ones that the other bricks are measured from. This teaches us that Jewish daughters serve as a measuring stick for others. Their level of *tznius* is considered a good indication of how things should be.

It's interesting to note that in the wall of a building, the corner stones are not in the center. Quite the opposite, they are at the far ends of the wall. So even though a Jewish daughter's *tznius* is a model for others, she doesn't have to push herself in the center of all the attention. Her standard will be noticed and compared to, wherever she may be found, even at the sidelines. This, too, is an expression of *tznius*.

Chavie lives in New York, but spends her summers working in Jewish day camps around the country. In her senior year she worked in Texas. One Sunday afternoon, Chavie and her co-counselors took advantage of the free afternoon to stock up on arts and crafts supplies.

"Let's walk to the store," Chavie suggested. "I had a big lunch and it would do me well to walk it off." Everyone agreed. The seven girls took to the road under the hot Texas sun, dressed in stark contrast to the locals.

After a mile hike, they reached the store's parking lot. Making their way across the expanse, they approached the entrance doors eager for air conditioning.

"Hey, y'all girls", they heard a woman's voice with the distinct southern drawl.

Chavie and her friends turned to the woman questioningly.

"Waitin' here for my ride, I've been watching y'all marchin' across that there lot," she said coming towards them. "I say, in those, them clothing you wearing in this heat and that, there innocent look you got about you - you must be G-d's children, now ain't you?"

We are not merely unto ourselves. Our *tznius* is a reflection of who we are as well as where we come from. Practicing proper *tznius* "in the meantime" - even as we are working on ourselves to do it right - can bring much *nachas* and joy to our families, schools, and communities. We have a responsibility to uphold their reputation, even while we are working at making a good name for ourselves.

We learn this from Boaz, the judge of Israel. When Boaz went out to the field and saw Ruth, he noticed how *tznius* she was and asked: לְמִי הַנַּעֲרָה הַזֹּאת -"To whom is this girl?" (*Ruth* 2:5).

Now, if he had wanted to know who she was he could have just said, "Who is this girl?" But Boaz was not merely asking for her name. He had noticed her *tznius* and wanted to know to whom she belonged. Who was the family, and who were the people, that taught this girl this impressive commitment to *tznius*?

DEVORI DOESN'T LIKE TO HAVE TO LIVE UP TO OTHER PEOPLE'S EXPECTATIONS JUST BECAUSE SHE IS THE DAUGHTER OF A DISTINGUISHED RABBI. IS THIS RIGHT?

The late 1800's was a difficult time for the small Jewish community of Yerushalayim. Food was scarce, security was lacking, and illness was rampant. But the people who had come from afar to settle in Yerushalayim were not the type to give in to hardship. They were G-d fearing and determined to reestablish the glory of Yerushalayim.

Under the able leadership of Rabbi Shmuel Salanter, every effort was made to ensure *yiras shamayim* and *shemiras hamitzvos* as is befitting the holy city. Knowing that this would set the tone for the future of Eretz Yisrael, Rabbi Salanter insisted on a high standard in all areas. He constantly spoke of kedushah and tznius to the public, and took every measure to make sure that his own family practiced what he preached.

It was customary, in those days, for the women and girls to wrap themselves in a large shawl on top of their clothes. This ancient style, covering up the shape of the body, had been worn by women throughout the ages. One day, it came to Rabbi Shmuel's attention that one of his granddaughters had exchanged the shawl for a more modern look.

He hurried to his son's home and told him, "You must make sure that your daughter dresses in the proper way, as is our custom. Otherwise, I will have to go around to all the shuls in Yerushalayim and declare that this is not my desire and that I have directed you to correct this. It must be done or people will say, 'This new style must be with the Rav's consent - after all, his granddaughter dresses like that.'"

DOING IT RIGHT,
WITH AIDELKEIT

"My name is Aidel, but everyone was always telling me that I wasn't. They said:

> My laugh is too loud, I stick out in a crowd.
> My walk spells conceit, I should be more discreet.
> I should carefully choose, the language I use.
> My heels do disturb and I sit on the curb.
> My hair hangs too loose, I use too much mousse.
> I wear too many rings and an outfit that clings.
>
> One day I thought: This is a shame,
> I really should live up to my name
> Then in class we had to read this book
> And now people say I have an *aideler* look."

Aidel is a hard word to define. Many people say it means refined. But what is refined? Is it a matter of taste? Is it a matter of opinion? What if some people are sensitive to some look and behavior and others are not? Indeed in some places people have become so desensitized to *aidelkeit* and *tznius* that they cannot see anything lacking in people's appearances and behavior.

Once a group of people confronted the Gerer Rebbe claiming that the standards of tznius were unrealistic and too old fashioned. "You have to live with the times," they claimed. "Maybe in the past people were not as confident and secure and could have been affected by what they saw in the streets. But look at us. We don't follow these guidelines and we're doing just fine. Do you really think that people are so primitive?"

The Rebbe was not intimidated by their words. He patiently replied, "You know, here in Israel, it is not uncommon to encounter a wandering Bedouin tending his herd. He walks about the hot trails barefoot, unaffected by pebbles and thorns, while we do not venture out on paved sidewalks without shoes. Yet who is considered more primitive?"

Being sensitive to that which is coarse and unrefined, is being aidel. Our Sages have brought to our attention some of the areas we should pay attention to as we strive for a tznius way of life.

The Talmud says: בִּשְׁלוֹשָׁה דְבָרִים אָדָם נִיכַּר בְּכוֹסוֹ וּבְכִיסוֹ וּבְכַעֲסוֹ וְאַמְרֵי לָהּ אַף בִּשְׂחָקוֹ "A person's true character is recognizable in the [following] three ways: the way he drinks [wine], how he spends his money, and how he reacts when he is angered. Some say, also by the way he laughs" (*Eruvin* 65b). You can see from the words in Hebrew, כּוֹסוֹ, כִּיסוֹ and כַּעֲסוֹ, that the first three things mentioned all have letters in common. Using this play on words, our Sages are teaching us about man's character. Yet, they added the last point about laughter, even if the Hebrew word בִּשְׂחָקוֹ seems out of place. It may not share the same letters, but the idea is similar.

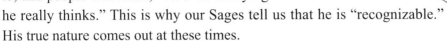

A person who is angry or drunk has a hard time controlling himself. But he must, because if he doesn't, he might say things that he hadn't intended to, and people will think, "Now he is saying what he really thinks." This is why our Sages tell us that he is "recognizable." His true nature comes out at these times.

A person who bursts out in raucous laughter or screams with hilarity at the top of her voice can be considered out of control. This is not in line with *tznius,* since *tznius* is a constant awareness and sensitivity to our appearance and behavior. This doesn't mean that we should walk around in a gloom! Most of us can clearly see the difference between a hearty laugh and unruly overexcited hysterics. We can show sincere and honest happiness at a time of joy without shouting at the top of our lungs.

Perhaps this is what our Sages meant when they said: דֶּרֶךְ בְּנוֹת יִשְׂרָאֵל לֹא פּוֹרְצוֹת בִּשְׂחוֹק- "Jewish girls do not burst out in laughter" (*Midrash Tanchuma, Naso* 2). This does not mean that we should not be happy. Aren't we commanded: עִבְדוּ אֶת ה' בְּשִׂמְחָה - "Serve *Hashem* with joy" (*Tehillim* 100:2)? Hasn't Shlomoh *haMelech* written: עֵת לִבְכּוֹת וְעֵת לִשְׂחוֹק - "A time to cry, a time to laugh" (*Koheles* 3:4)? Yet our Sages say: "They do not *burst out....*" The Hebrew word for "burst out" is פּוֹרְצוֹת, which is the same word that is used when describing the opposite of *tznius* - פְּרִיצוּת. We express our happiness in ways that compliment our *tznius.*

When Shlomoh *haMelech* praises the Jewish woman in *Eishes Chayil*, he says: פִּיהָ פָּתְחָה בְחָכְמָה - "She opens her mouth with wisdom" (*Mishlei* 31:26). With this, he means that she speaks calmly and peacefully, as wise people do: דִּבְרֵי חֲכָמִים בְּנַחַת נִשְׁמָעִים "The wise express themselves calmly" (*Koheles* 9:17).

WHAT IF I AM BY NATURE AN EXUBERANT PERSON? SHOULD I SUPPRESS MY NATURE?

In addition to the way we talk, tznius in speech includes what we say. People were commenting to Aidel that she should be careful in her choice of words. We can learn from the Torah to be particular in the way we speak and to choose our words with care. When

Noach was commanded to take the animals into the ark, *Hashem* said: בְּהֵמָה אֲשֶׁר לֹא טְהֹרָה הִיא - "the animal that is not *tahor*" (*Bereishis* 7:2). Why did *Hashem* say "not *tahor*"? He could have just said "*tamei*," which has the same meaning. However, since it was possible to use a more refined term, *Hashem* did so.

With the tremendous lack of *tznius* all around us it may seem less important to pay close attention to our speech. There is so much to pay attention to and improve. Yet when *Hashem* made this choice of words it was just before the *mabul*. The world was in an awful state, including a terrible lack of *tznius*, and it was all going to be destroyed. Even at a time like that, care was taken to use refined speech.

Maybe a lack of proper speech is actually where the trouble starts. If we would be careful not to use language that is not *aidel*, it would be easier to stay away from behavior and clothes that are not appropriate.

Our Sages point this out when they list the merits of the Jewish people in *Galus Mitzrayim*. לֹא שִׁינוּ אֶת לְשׁוֹנָם - "they did not change their speech." In addition to making the effort to speak in Hebrew, they were careful not to speak the street language of the Egyptians.

It is not so surprising then that David *haMelech* gives the following description of a Jew's speech: הוּצַק חֵן בְּשִׂפְתוֹתֶיךָ עַל כֵּן בֵּרַכְךָ אֱלֹקִים לְעוֹלָם - "*Chein* pours from your lips; therefore *Hashem* blesses you forever" (*Tehillim* 45:3). When people want to describe a graceful and charming person they say: "That person has *Yiddishe chein*." David *haMelech* teaches us that *aidelkeit* in our speech will not only contribute to our charm and gracefulness, but will bring us blessings.

CAN THERE BE DIFFERENT PHRASES, MANNERS OF SPEECH, OR OTHER AREAS OF TZNIUS THAT MAY BE ACCEPTABLE IN ONE LOCALE BUT FROWNED UPON IN ANOTHER?

Another thing we should consider when we talk is to whom we are speaking. It is not *tznius* for men and women to speak to each other unnecessarily. We should be careful not to have conversations that are uncalled for. This has always been the manner in which Jewish men and women, boys and girls, have conducted themselves. The Talmud (*Eruvin* 53b) tells us of a scholar who was reprimanded by Beruria, the learned wife of Rabbi Meir.

The scholar encountered her and asked her, "Which way do we go to get to Lod (a city in Israel)?" Beruria showed him, but added that it would have been more appropriate to ask: "Which, to Lod?" That would have been enough for her to understand the question and limit the conversation.

People told Aidel that she draws too much attention to herself and sticks out too much in a crowd. Sure, we like to be among people. We like when they notice our presence and accomplishments. Yet, a person whose way of life is tznius doesn't rely on the public to constantly reassure her that she is appreciated. She doesn't need to have her successes seen by everyone. She is modest and humble and she reassures herself by looking inside for strength.

Humility and modesty have always been the Jewish way. No one but Avraham and Yitzchak witnessed their great test at the *Akeidah*. No one but Yaakov stayed at that critical time when he overcame the *malach* of Esav and was given the title of "Father of *Bnei Yisrael*." No one but Moshe Rabbeinu was there when *Hashem* appeared to him and appointed him the leader and redeemer of *Am Yisrael*. No one but the *Kohen Gadol* himself stood by to see how a human being serves *Hashem* in the holiest place on earth where the *Shechinah* is most present.

The Rebbe of Stretin, Rabbi Avraham, had a very righteous daughter. Her dress, speech and manners were an example of extreme aidelkeit and tznius. She cared deeply for others and constantly prayed for their well-being. In time, it became known that her prayers were answered. People spoke of her with awe and admiration.

But this refined woman was far from pleased. One evening, she was so troubled by this attention that she decided then and there to move away for awhile, hoping to be forgotten by the local people. That night, she packed her belongings in two large suitcases, and in the early morning she took her two children to the train station. After a few hours of travel, they arrived in the city of Lemberg.

It was then, in the hustle and bustle of the strange, large city, that the young

mother began to collect her thoughts. "What shall I do? In my haste to get away from all that recognition, I did not plan this journey properly. Where shall I go from here?" She looked around, her dismay growing as she was overwhelmed by the surging crowd.

Suddenly she heard a familiar voice calling her name. She turned around and saw a women motioning to her. It was the woman who used to cook in her house years ago. "Come with me," she said. The woman helped her with her luggage and led her to a quiet part of town where the weary travelers were welcomed into a lovely inn.

"It's all arranged," the woman told her. "You can stay for as long as you wish."

The guests were tended to graciously by the staff and soon settled down comfortably. But when the grateful woman looked around to thank her former cook, she was nowhere to be found. Suddenly, she trembled in fear. "My former cook," she whispered to herself, "passed away about five years ago...."

Some time later, when the Rebbe's daughter returned to her home in Stretin, she related the entire incident to her father. "That woman was sent to you from above to assist you in your time of need," he said. "You merited this because of your dedication to a life of tznius. That cook also conducted herself in the same way, and that is why help from heaven came through her image."

Being *tznius* means setting a Torah standard for the way we present ourselves. We don't need to rely on applause and acceptance that comes from the outside. Self-confidence comes from the inside. Let's live up to our title as a king's daughter with pride, joy and determination!

OUR RABBIS TEACH

אֶשְׁתְּךָ כְּגֶפֶן פֹּרִיָּה בְּיַרְכְּתֵי בֵיתֶךָ - "Your wife is like a fruitful vine in the inner chambers of your home" (*Tehillim* 128:3).

A Jewish woman is compared to grapes. When we squeeze grapes to make wine, we are cautious with the juice. We make sure it is covered and protected so its quality will not be compromised. This way, the wine we produce will have a very good flavor. A Jewish woman is also compared to tasty wine, which is a symbol of joy and festivity. Just as wine is not left out in the open, so too, our best qualities develop as we follow the protective guidelines for a *tznius* way of life.

In the Talmud (*Midrash Tanchuma, Parashas Vayishlach*, sec. 5), in the midst of a discussion on the laws of Shabbos, the question is asked about a particular piece of jewelry. This piece, known as "the city of gold" was a fancy ornament that was worn at that time. Because it was not part of the clothing, there was a question whether one would be permitted to go out wearing it on Shabbos or whether it was forbidden because it would be considered carrying. Our Sages declare: Go out wearing it on Shabbos?! Even on a weekday a woman should not go out wearing such a showy piece! That would not be in line with *tznius*. A woman should wear her nicest jewelry at home, dressing up for the people who count most in her life.

Our Sages tell us that women would weave the פָּרֹכֶת, the special curtains that hung in the *Beis haMikdash*. Why were the women chosen to do this skillful job? The פָּרֹכֶת was hung between the קֹדֶשׁ and the קֹדֶשׁ הַקֳּדָשִׁים, keeping the אֲרוֹן הַבְּרִית - the Ark of the Covenant - separate and private. It was like a partition of *tznius,* telling us that something holy is inside. With every expert stroke that fastened the delicate threads onto the weaving loom, the women firmly connected themselves to a lifelong dedication to *tznius*.

This bond between *tznius*, women, and the פָּרֹכֶת continued after the *Beis haMikdash* was destroyed. In our shuls, an attractive פָּרֹכֶת hangs in front of the אֲרוֹן קֹדֶשׁ. Women were accustomed to wear long flowing dresses made of durable high-quality fabric. In their old age, they donated these dresses to the shul, and the פָּרֹכֶת, which hangs on the אֲרוֹן קֹדֶשׁ, was sewn from them.

Rabbi Yissachar Dov of Belz, would begin his Yom Kippur *davening* by standing reverently before the אֲרוֹן קֹדֶשׁ. He spoke with great emotion of his righteous grandmother from whose dress the פָּרֹכֶת hanging before him was made. He pleaded that *Hashem* accept the prayers of the Jewish people on this holy day in the merit of the dedicated women who lived a life of *tznius* and educated their children to follow in their footsteps.

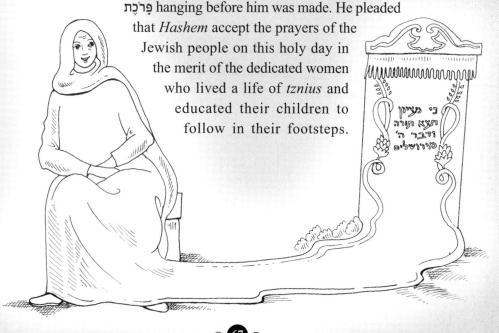

בָּנֶיךָ כִּשְׁתִלֵי זֵיתִים סָבִיב לְשֻׁלְחָנֶךָ - "Your children are like olive branches around your table" (*Tehillim* 128:3).

In agriculture, branches from one tree can be attached to another type of tree in a way that the connected branch grows onto the new tree. This is called grafting. But an olive branch doesn't graft. It just won't grow on any other tree. Olive oil does not mix easily with water; it rises to the top. Jewish children are compared to olive branches. They are careful to live up to a high standard. They grow and develop from their own home base - "around *your* table." They do not mingle in outside circles that are improper. The *tznius* way of life guides them.

וְעָשׂוּ לִי מִקְדָּשׁ וְשָׁכַנְתִּי בְּתוֹכָם - "And you will make for me a sanctuary, and I will dwell among them" (*Shemos* 25:8).

Hashem wants this world to be a home for Him, a place where His holiness can dwell. He commanded us to build the *Mishkan* in a way that it would be a proper home for His *Shechinah*. The *Mishkan* had no permanent roof; it was covered with woven rugs that hung over the top. Our Sages compare this to a modestly dressed woman, whose dress is long enough and whose head is covered properly. In this *pasuk Hashem* says: "I will dwell among them." Our *tznius* provides a proper setting for the *Shechinah* to settle within us.

Just my style

FUN PAGES

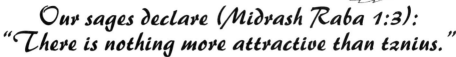

אֵין לְךָ יָפֶה מִן הַצְּנִיעוּת

Our sages declare (Midrash Raba 1:3): "There is nothing more attractive than tznius."

Throughout the ages and though dispersed to all corners of the globe, Jewish women are united by their ongoing commitment to tznius as their way of life. Identify the country of origin of each woman.

16th century
Germany

18th century
France

Ancient Greece

19th century
Scotland

Early 20th
century Jerusalem

Ukraine
countryside

The girls on this page are inspired by Ruth to pay more attention to tznius. Miriam stoops properly to pick up her ball. Michal's skirt covers amply as she sits. Shoshanah checks her top button. Yael's sleeves don't ride up above her elbows as she erases the board. Gila chooses an aidel pair of shoes.

Put yourself in the picture. Draw an area of tznius that you can improve upon.

18th century Hungary

19th century Russia

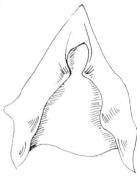

20th century
Morroco

אֵשֶׁת חַיִל עֲטֶרֶת בַּעְלָה

A Jewish woman who dresses and acts *tznius* and covers her hair properly is the crowning glory of her husband. Around the world and throughout the ages Jewish women have worn this title with joy and dedication. Match the outfit to the headpiece.

18th century America

20th century
Island of Rhodes

כַּלָּה נָאָה וַחֲסוּדָה

An attractive and graceful bride

Following in the footsteps of Rivkah Imeinu, a bride's face is covered with a veil as an expression of *tznius*. Find 10 differences in the two wedding pictures.

On the path of our ancestors

The following hints will help you fill the puzzle with names of women and men in the *tanach*

The name of *Hashem* throughout the world he spread,
But modestly, "I am dust and ashes," he said.

Teaching women about *Hashem*, her time was spent,
And this she did modestly, from inside her tent.

Blessed with success in the seeds he had sown,
He was modest, not anxious to make his wealth known.

Righteous and gracious, kind and polite,
She wrapped up modestly, when her groom was in sight.

He said, "My sons, don't stand out or you'll be detected;
Keep a low, modest profile, and you'll be protected."

She was meant to be the first wife, everyone knew.
Modestly, she kept the secret; to her sister she was true.

Blessed with six sons, she modestly thought of others,
"Please *Hashem*, let this baby be a sister to her brothers."

He was bothered and pestered, but to no avail.
Because of his modesty, he was thrown in jail.

Though holy and shining from the moment of birth,
He was the most modest of all people upon the face of the earth.

Though he did not know it, his own life he did save,
Due to modesty, when he went deep in the cave.

The words of *Tehillim,* read daily by all -
How modest the writer who claims he's so small.

She had to kill Sisra, she swiftly had him floored,
But it's not modest for women, so she didn't use a sword.

All the girls ordered makeup to enhance their beauty,
But she asked for nothing - modesty was her duty.

Gleaning in the field, her modesty was praised;
From heartache and hunger, to royalty she was raised.

Seven sons - high priests, a merit quite rare,
Due to her modest way of covering her hair.

Identify the girls

Rina is standing to the left of the girl whose belt is not oversized and showy. Bina, whose earrings do not dangle too long, is standing to Rina's left. She is wearing a proper neckline, but different from one that buttons up to the top.

Dina likes to wear bracelets, but she doesn't wear too many at a time. She is not speaking to the girl whose hair is tied neatly.

The girl whose elbow and midriff are not revealed when she raises her hand is not calling Pnina. However, Pnina is near the girl whose headband is placed neatly away from her forehead.

Nina is the type of girl who is particular that her school bag looks and is worn in a dignified manner. She is close to Rina who chooses to stand, rather than sit on the sidewalk and lean against the wall, while waiting for the bus.

Yonina is not near Adina but they both like to wear tailored clothes, yet are careful that slits are sewn up and shirts are not tight fitted.

Mina is to the right of Rina but left of Yonina, and she could see that Rina, Bina, Dina, Pnina, Nina, Adina and Yonina are all sensitive to a tzinus appearance.

_____   _____   _____   _____   _____   _____   _____   _____

Girls speak about tznius

Who is saying:

1. *Tznius* makes me think
2. *Tznius* is just my style!
3. Sometimes *tznius* can be hard
4. *Tznius* suits me just fine
5. *Tznius* makes me feel regal
6. I look up to people who are *tznius*
7. *Tznius* can be frustrating
8. *Tznius* requires inner strength

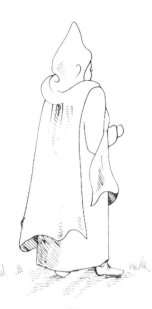

כֹּה תֹאמַר לְבֵית יַעֲקֹב - אֵלוּ הַנָשִׁים

"The house of Yaakov -
these are the women"
(Shemos Rabbah 28)

Turkey

England

A woman is called עֲקֶרֶת הַבַּיִת. She creates the atmosphere in the home. For centuries, Jewish women have been devoted to illuminating their homes with warmth and holiness.

Match the woman to her home.

Jerusalem

Usbekistan

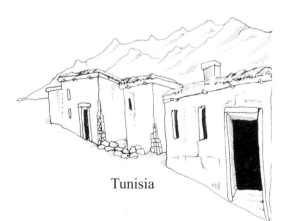
Tunisia